GOD'S
GRACE

for

—

LEADERS

B&H
PUBLISHING GROUP
NASHVILLE, TENNESSEE

Copyright © 2018 by B&H Publishing Group
All Rights Reserved
Printed in the United States of America

978-1-5359-1751-3

Published by B&H Publishing Group
Nashville, Tennessee

Dewey Decimal Classification: 234.1
Subject Heading: GRACE (THEOLOGY) / HOPE / SELF-CONFIDENCE

All Scripture quotations are taken from the Christian Standard Bible®, copyright
© 2017 by Holman Bible Publishers. Used by permission. Christian Standard
Bible® and CSB® are federally registered trademarks of Holman Bible Publishers.

1 2 3 4 5 6 7 8 · 22 21 20 19 18

CONTENTS

INTRODUCTION

Life tends to maneuver us into categories, into penciled-in bubbles on the random identification form. Some of them we like; some we don't. Some we actively seek out and continue to pursue; some are sitting there waiting for us and won't turn us loose.

But one thing we all know: deep inside these simple boxes and check marks reside entire worlds crawling with complication, challenge, and difficulty. Even if easy to get into, they are rarely so easy to faithfully, successfully, and steadily keep going through.

As a leader, for instance, you may often feel inadequate to the tasks on you or ahead of you. No matter what the role, the burden of leadership is never light. Your days are likely full of activity yet can still feel unfinished. You try maximizing the jobs your particular box (or boxes) entails, yet they maddeningly resist being colored all the way to the edges.

The reason this book exists is because God's grace never met a check box it couldn't fill with hope, peace, direction, and perspective—with motivation, counsel, freedom, and opportunity. This book is here, and is now yours, because the Bible not only speaks timelessly to everyone but specifically to you . . . with grace. God's grace. Sufficient to every place. Even to the places you're living this very moment.

ANGER

As a leader, your ability to properly manage and channel your anger sets an example for those you lead—be sure you speak and act with love.

❧

Refrain from anger and give up your rage;
do not be agitated—it can only bring harm.
　　　Psalm 37:8

❧

A patient person shows great understanding,
but a quick-tempered one promotes foolishness.
　　　Proverbs 14:29

❧

A gentle answer turns away anger,
but a harsh word stirs up wrath.
　　　Proverbs 15:1

"But I tell you, everyone who is angry with his brother or sister will be subject to judgment. Whoever insults his brother or sister, will be subject to the court. Whoever says, 'You fool!' will be subject to hellfire."
    Matthew 5:22

∽

Be angry and do not sin. Don't let the sun go down on your anger, and don't give the devil an opportunity.
    Ephesians 4:26–27

∽

*Lord, may Your Holy Spirit guide my
words and actions when I'm feeling angry
so that I can lead by a godly example.*

ANXIETY

Beneath our anxieties is the need to feel in control of our circumstances—but our peace is found in remembering that all things work together for the good of those who love God.

"Therefore I tell you: Don't worry about your life, what you will eat or what you will drink; or about your body, what you will wear. Isn't life more than food and the body more than clothing? Consider the birds of the sky: They don't sow or reap or gather into barns, yet your heavenly Father feeds them. Aren't you worth more than they? Can any of you add one moment to his life-span by worrying?"
    Matthew 6:25–27

"Peace I leave with you. My peace I give to you. I do not give to you as the world gives. Don't let your heart be troubled or fearful."
    John 14:27

Don't worry about anything, but in everything, through prayer and petition with thanksgiving, present your requests to God. And the peace of God, which surpasses all understanding, will guard your hearts and minds in Christ Jesus.

Philippians 4:6–7

For God has not given us a spirit of fear, but one of power, love, and sound judgment.

2 Timothy 1:7

Humble yourselves, therefore, under the mighty hand of God, so that he may exalt you at the proper time, casting all your cares on him, because he cares about you.

1 Peter 5:6–7

Heavenly Father, I entrust to You my family, my work, my church, and the people who look to me for leadership—may Your peace guard my heart and mind.

AUTHORITY

As a leader, you hold an important position of authority—seek wisdom in all your decisions from God, who is ultimately in control of every sphere of life.

∽

Then he said to them, "Give, then, to Caesar the things that are Caesar's, and to God the things that are God's." When they heard this, they were amazed. So they left him and went away.
    Matthew 22:21–22

∽

Jesus came near and said to them, "All authority has been given to me in heaven and on earth."
    Matthew 28:18

∽

Let everyone submit to the governing authorities, since there is no authority except from God, and the authorities that exist are instituted by God.
    Romans 13:1

*For this reason God highly exalted him
and gave him the name
that is above every name,
so that at the name of Jesus
every knee will bow—
in heaven and on earth
and under the earth—
and every tongue will confess
that Jesus Christ is Lord,
to the glory of God the Father.*
    Philippians 2:9–11

*Submit to every human authority because of the Lord, whether to the
emperor as the supreme authority or to governors as those sent out
by him to punish those who do what is evil and to praise those who do
what is good. For it is God's will that you silence the ignorance of foolish
people by doing good.*
    1 Peter 2:13–15

*Dear Jesus, I praise You for granting me wisdom and
grace to be a mirror of godly authority to others, and
I willingly submit to Your authority in all things.*

BLESSINGS

We can experience deep joy when we take notice of the abundant blessings in our lives and praise and thank the Lord for such bountiful grace.

∽

"May the LORD bless you and protect you; may the LORD make his face shine on you and be gracious to you; may the LORD look with favor on you and give you peace."
    Numbers 6:24–26

∽

Indeed, we have all received grace upon grace from his fullness, for the law was given through Moses; grace and truth came through Jesus Christ.
    John 1:16–17

And God is able to make every grace overflow to you, so that in every way, always having everything you need, you may excel in every good work.
    2 Corinthians 9:8

Blessed is the God and Father of our Lord Jesus Christ, who has blessed us with every spiritual blessing in the heavens in Christ.
    Ephesians 1:3

And my God will supply all your needs according to his riches in glory in Christ Jesus.
    Philippians 4:19

*Heavenly Father, thank You and praise
You for all the ways You have blessed me,
most of all with the gift of Your own Son.*

CARING

A godly leader isn't one who seeks power or advancement but cares for the people around them as Jesus, the Good Shepherd, cares for His church.

❧

"I give you a new command: Love one another. Just as I have loved you, you are also to love one another. By this everyone will know that you are my disciples, if you love one another."
    John 13:34–35

❧

Carry one another's burdens; in this way you will fulfill the law of Christ.
    Galatians 6:2

*Therefore, as we have opportunity, let us work for the good of all,
especially for those who belong to the household of faith.*
    Galatians 6:10

*Everyone should look out not only for his own interests, but also for the
interests of others.*
    Philippians 2:4

*Dear Jesus, grant me the opportunity to
extend caring and compassion to those I
encounter who may need encouragement today.*

CHANGE

Leading a group, school, organization, or movement is fraught with ongoing change and uncertainty, but you can rest in the promise that Christ is the same yesterday, today, and forever.

There is an occasion for everything, and a time for every activity under heaven.
    Ecclesiastes 3:1

"Do not remember the past events, pay no attention to things of old. Look, I am about to do something new; even now it is coming. Do you not see it? Indeed, I will make a way in the wilderness, rivers in the desert."
    Isaiah 43:18–19

"Because I, the LORD, have not changed, you descendants of Jacob have not been destroyed."
    Malachi 3:6

❧

Therefore, if anyone is in Christ, he is a new creation; the old has passed away, and see, the new has come!
    2 Corinthians 5:17

❧

Jesus Christ is the same yesterday, today, and forever.
    Hebrews 13:8

❧

Lord Jesus, no matter what the future
brings, may I take heart that You are
with me until the end of the age.

COMPASSION

Jesus instructs us to love our neighbors as ourselves and also love our enemies—we demonstrate compassionate leadership by acting in the best interests of others.

❧

Yet he was compassionate;
he atoned for their iniquity
and did not destroy them.
He often turned his anger aside
and did not unleash all his wrath.
  Psalm 78:38

❧

When he went ashore, he saw a large crowd and had compassion on them, because they were like sheep without a shepherd. Then he began to teach them many things.
  Mark 6:34

Carry one another's burdens; in this way you will fulfill the law of Christ.
   Galatians 6:2

∽

And be kind and compassionate to one another, forgiving one another, just as God also forgave you in Christ.
   Ephesians 4:32

∽

Lord, may Your Holy Spirit fill my heart and soul with concern for those who depend on my leadership so that I may be a willing conduit of Your love.

CONFIDENCE

Rising to leadership and its various challenges may test your confidence, but remember that the power that created the universe and raised Christ from the dead lives inside of you.

Do not fear, for I am with you;
do not be afraid, for I am your God.
I will strengthen you; I will help you;
I will hold on to you with my righteous right hand.
    Isaiah 41:10

It is not that we are competent in ourselves to claim anything as coming from ourselves, but our adequacy is from God.
    2 Corinthians 3:5

I am able to do all things through him who strengthens me.
Philippians 4:13

So don't throw away your confidence, which has a great reward. For you need endurance, so that after you have done God's will, you may receive what was promised.
Hebrews 10:35–36

This is how we will know that we belong to the truth and will reassure our hearts before him whenever our hearts condemn us; for God is greater than our hearts, and he knows all things. Dear friends, if our hearts don't condemn us, we have confidence before God and receive whatever we ask from him because we keep his commands and do what is pleasing in his sight.
1 John 3:19–22

Heavenly Father, grant me inner strength and confidence as I trust You to provide everything I need to excel in the good work You have given me to do.

CONFLICT

We can walk in the Spirit, rather than according to the flesh, by resisting pride and the need to be right that we often feel in conflicts with others.

Bless those who persecute you; bless and do not curse. Rejoice with those who rejoice; weep with those who weep. Live in harmony with one another. Do not be proud; instead, associate with the humble. Do not be wise in your own estimation. Do not repay anyone evil for evil. Give careful thought to do what is honorable in everyone's eyes. If possible, as far as it depends on you, live at peace with everyone.
    Romans 12:14–18

"If your brother sins against you, go and rebuke him in private. If he listens to you, you have won your brother. But if he won't listen, take one or two others with you, so that by the testimony of two or three witnesses every fact may be established. If he doesn't pay attention to them, tell the church. If he doesn't pay attention even to the church, let him be like a Gentile and a tax collector to you."
    Matthew 18:15–17

Therefore, putting away lying, speak the truth, each one to his neighbor, because we are members of one another. Be angry and do not sin. Don't let the sun go down on your anger, and don't give the devil an opportunity.

    Ephesians 4:25–27

A gentle answer turns away anger, but a harsh word stirs up wrath.

    Proverbs 15:1

What is the source of wars and fights among you? Don't they come from your passions that wage war within you? You desire and do not have. You murder and covet and cannot obtain. You fight and wage war. You do not have because you do not ask.

    James 4:1–2

Lord Jesus, may I imitate Your grace and gentleness in any disagreement or confrontation with my family, colleagues, and those under my leadership.

COURAGE

Having courage doesn't mean you feel no fear—rather it means you're willing and ready to proceed despite the fear.

ɔ⁄ɔ

"Haven't I commanded you: be strong and courageous? Do not be afraid or discouraged, for the LORD your God is with you wherever you go."
   Joshua 1:9

ɔ⁄ɔ

I always let the LORD guide me.
Because he is at my right hand,
I will not be shaken.
   Psalm 16:8

Wait for the LORD;
be strong, and let your heart be courageous.
Wait for the LORD.
     Psalm 27:14

∽

Be alert, stand firm in the faith, be courageous, be strong.
     1 Corinthians 16:13

∽

For God has not given us a spirit of fear, but one of power, love, and
sound judgment.
     2 Timothy 1:7

∽

Dear God, please grant me Your
strength and presence so that I may face
this day and its challenges with courage.

CREATIVITY

Being made in the image of God means that every person is also endowed with the creativity of the Creator.

So God created man in his own image; he created him in the image of God; he created them male and female.
    Genesis 1:27

I will praise you
because I have been remarkably and wondrously made.
Your works are wondrous,
and I know this very well.
    Psalm 139:14

Do you see a person skilled in his work?
He will stand in the presence of kings.
He will not stand in the presence of the unknown.
      Proverbs 22:29

⁓

All things were created through him, and apart from him not one thing
was created that has been created.
      John 1:3

⁓

For we are his workmanship, created in Christ Jesus for good works,
which God prepared ahead of time for us to do.
      Ephesians 2:10

⁓

Lord Jesus, through whom all things were
made, guide my mind, heart, and hands to create
goodness and beauty in every area of my life.

DEPRESSION

When your heart is heavy and your mind is burdened, hold fast to the truth that God comforts us in all of our afflictions so that we may be able to comfort others with His love.

The LORD sits enthroned over the flood;
the LORD sits enthroned, King forever.
The LORD gives his people strength;
the LORD blesses his people with peace.
        Psalm 29:10–11

"Do not fear, for I am with you;
do not be afraid, for I am your God.
I will strengthen you; I will help you;
I will hold on to you with my righteous right hand."
        Isaiah 41:10

The LORD is near the brokenhearted;
he saves those crushed in spirit.
    Psalm 34:18

Answer me quickly, LORD;
my spirit fails.
Don't hide your face from me,
or I will be like those
going down to the Pit.
Let me experience
your faithful love in the morning,
for I trust in you.
Reveal to me the way I should go
because I appeal to you.
    Psalm 143:7–8

Dear Jesus, You were a man of sorrows and
acquainted with grief—please fill my heart with
Your strength and bring me peace.

DISCERNMENT

The Holy Spirit is our ever-present Helper who grants us wisdom so that we can lead according to the perfect will of God.

So give your servant a receptive heart to judge your people and to discern between good and evil. For who is able to judge this great people of yours?
        1 Kings 3:9

And I pray this: that your love will keep on growing in knowledge and every kind of discernment, so that you may approve the things that are superior and may be pure and blameless in the day of Christ.
        Philippians 1:9–10

Don't stifle the Spirit. Don't despise prophecies, but test all things. Hold on to what is good. Stay away from every kind of evil.
    1 Thessalonians 5:19–22

❧

Now if any of you lacks wisdom, he should ask God—who gives to all generously and ungrudgingly—and it will be given to him.
    James 1:5

❧

Dear friends, do not believe every spirit, but test the spirits to see if they are from God, because many false prophets have gone out into the world.
    1 John 4:1

❧

Holy Spirit, may I be open and receptive to Your prompting so that I discern what is right and good in all things.

DISCIPLINE

A godly leader cultivates self-discipline by doing the right thing at the right time in the right way.

Whoever loves discipline loves knowledge,
but one who hates correction is stupid.
    Proverbs 12:1

The one who will not use the rod hates his son,
but the one who loves him disciplines him diligently.
    Proverbs 13:24

Foolishness is bound to the heart of a youth;
a rod of discipline will separate it from him.
    Proverbs 22:15

Instead, I discipline my body and bring it under strict control, so that after preaching to others, I myself will not be disqualified.
   1 Corinthians 9:27

No discipline seems enjoyable at the time, but painful. Later on, however, it yields the peaceful fruit of righteousness to those who have been trained by it.
   Hebrews 12:11

Heavenly Father, may Your hand guide me and correct me so that all I do and say will glorify You.

DISCOURAGEMENT

When the day feels endless and our tasks never-ending, we can call on the God of hope to fill us with joy, peace, and strength.

∾

The LORD is the one who will go before you. He will be with you; he will not leave you or abandon you. Do not be afraid or discouraged.
   Deuteronomy 31:8

∾

"I have told you these things so that in me you may have peace. You will have suffering in this world. Be courageous! I have conquered the world."
   John 16:33

∾

Now may the God of hope fill you with all joy and peace as you believe so that you may overflow with hope by the power of the Holy Spirit.
   Romans 15:13

In the same way the Spirit also helps us in our weakness, because we do not know what to pray for as we should, but the Spirit himself intercedes for us with unspoken groanings. And he who searches our hearts knows the mind of the Spirit, because he intercedes for the saints according to the will of God. We know that all things work together for the good of those who love God, who are called according to his purpose.
    Romans 8:26–28

But he said to me, "My grace is sufficient for you, for my power is perfected in weakness."
Therefore, I will most gladly boast all the more about my weaknesses, so that Christ's power may reside in me.
    2 Corinthians 12:9

Lord, sometimes it's hard to remember that You're in control of all things—please grant me Your grace and strength in this moment of discouragement.

ENCOURAGEMENT

Leaders can find deep gladness in knowing that our God goes before us and is with us at all times.

The LORD is the one who will go before you. He will be with you; he will not leave you or abandon you. Do not be afraid or discouraged.
    Deuteronomy 31:8

God is our refuge and strength,
a helper who is always found
in times of trouble.
    Psalm 46:1

"Aren't five sparrows sold for two pennies? Yet not one of them is forgotten in God's sight. Indeed, the hairs of your head are all counted. Don't be afraid; you are worth more than many sparrows."
    Luke 12:6–7

"I have told you these things so that in me you may have peace. You will have suffering in this world. Be courageous! I have conquered the world."

    John 16:33

✍

And let us watch out for one another to provoke love and good works, not neglecting to gather together, as some are in the habit of doing, but encouraging each other, and all the more as you see the day approaching.

    Hebrews 10:24–25

✍

Christ Jesus, may Your Spirit strengthen and encourage my heart today so that I am a source of encouragement to those under my leadership.

FAILURE

Though failures of any kind can crush our spirits, we have the assurance that God's purposes can never be thwarted.

❧

A person's steps are established by the LORD,
and he takes pleasure in his way.
Though he falls, he will not be overwhelmed,
because the LORD supports him with his hand.
    Psalm 37:23–24

❧

He brought me up from a desolate pit,
out of the muddy clay,
and set my feet on a rock,
making my steps secure.
He put a new song in my mouth,
a hymn of praise to our God.
Many will see and fear,
and they will trust in the LORD.
    Psalm 40:2–3

*And not only that, but we also rejoice in our afflictions, because we
know that affliction produces endurance, endurance produces proven
character, and proven character produces hope.*
    Romans 5:3–4

℘

*Now we have this treasure in clay jars, so that this extraordinary power
may be from God and not from us. We are afflicted in every way but not
crushed; we are perplexed but not in despair; we are persecuted but not
abandoned; we are struck down but not destroyed.*
    2 Corinthians 4:7–9

℘

*Brothers and sisters, I do not consider myself to have taken hold of it.
But one thing I do: Forgetting what is behind and reaching forward to
what is ahead, I pursue as my goal the prize promised by God's heavenly
call in Christ Jesus.*
    Philippians 3:13–14

℘

*Heavenly Father, grant me grace in times of failure
and help me press forward as I fix my eyes on Jesus.*

FAITHFULNESS

God's everlasting faithfulness to His people is a deep source of hope, as well as an inspiration for how we should conduct ourselves in our relationships.

Because of the LORD's faithful love
we do not perish,
for his mercies never end.
They are new every morning;
great is your faithfulness!
      Lamentations 3:22–23

"His master said to him, 'Well done, good and faithful servant! You were faithful over a few things; I will put you in charge of many things. Share your master's joy.'"
      Matthew 25:21

"Whoever is faithful in very little is also faithful in much, and whoever is unrighteous in very little is also unrighteous in much. So if you have not been faithful with worldly wealth, who will trust you with what is genuine? And if you have not been faithful with what belongs to someone else, who will give you what is your own?"
   Luke 16:10–12

If we are faithless, he remains faithful, for he cannot deny himself.
   2 Timothy 2:13

Let us hold on to the confession of our hope without wavering, since he who promised is faithful.
   Hebrews 10:23

Dear God, whose mercies are new every morning, grant me wisdom to be faithful to my family, church, and organization.

FAMILY

The heart of a leader is a source of love, wisdom, and encouragement for family members of all ages.

This is why a man leaves his father and mother and bonds with his wife, and they become one flesh.
Genesis 2:24

Wives, submit to your husbands as to the Lord, because the husband is the head of the wife as Christ is the head of the church. He is the Savior of the body. Now as the church submits to Christ, so also wives are to submit to their husbands in everything. Husbands, love your wives, just as Christ loved the church and gave himself for her to make her holy, cleansing her with the washing of water by the word. He did this to present the church to himself in splendor, without spot or wrinkle or anything like that, but holy and blameless. In the same way, husbands are to love their wives as their own bodies. He who loves his wife loves himself.
Ephesians 5:22–28

"Honor your father and your mother so that you may have a long life in the land that the LORD your God is giving you."
Exodus 20:12

✑

Sons are indeed a heritage from the LORD,
offspring, a reward.
Like arrows in the hand of a warrior
are the sons born in one's youth.
Happy is the man who has filled his quiver with them.
They will never be put to shame
when they speak with their enemies at the city gate.
Psalm 127:3–5

✑

Fathers, don't stir up anger in your children, but bring them up in the training and instruction of the Lord.
Ephesians 6:4

✑

Lord, thank You for how You demonstrate Your love and grace through my family and loved ones. May I be a reflection of Your love to them in all I do and say.

FEAR

Guiding people toward a shared vision and common goals can be a frightening prospect, but God commands us not to fear because He is with us and will help us in all our endeavors.

❧

"Haven't I commanded you: be strong and courageous? Do not be afraid or discouraged, for the LORD your God is with you wherever you go."
    Joshua 1:9

❧

When I am afraid,
I will trust in you.
    Psalm 56:3

❧

You did not receive a spirit of slavery to fall back into fear. Instead, you received the Spirit of adoption, by whom we cry out, "Abba, Father!"
    Romans 8:15

For God has not given us a spirit of fear, but one of power, love, and sound judgment.
   2 Timothy 1:7

⁓

Humble yourselves, therefore, under the mighty hand of God, so that he may exalt you at the proper time, casting all your cares on him, because he cares about you.
   1 Peter 5:6–7

⁓

Abba, Father, I call out to You for Your protection and comfort in moments when I'm afraid—thank You for Your faithful love and comfort.

FELLOWSHIP

As a leader working long hours and pulled in many directions, fellowship with other believers can refresh your heart and soul.

☙

Iron sharpens iron,
and one person sharpens another.
　　Proverbs 27:17

☙

Two are better than one because they have a good reward for their efforts. For if either falls, his companion can lift him up; but pity the one who falls without another to lift him up.
　　Ecclesiastes 4:9–10

☙

Carry one another's burdens; in this way you will fulfill the law of Christ.
　　Galatians 6:2

Therefore encourage one another and build each other up as you are already doing.
 1 Thessalonians 5:11

∾

And let us watch out for one another to provoke love and good works, not neglecting to gather together, as some are in the habit of doing, but encouraging each other, and all the more as you see the day approaching.
 Hebrews 10:24–25

∾

Dear Jesus, my heavenly Friend,
please show me ways I can spend more time in
fellowship with people who love and serve You.

FORGIVENESS

Forgiving someone who has wronged you means you no longer call to mind their fault or mistake—this gives grace to them and freedom to you.

✍

"Therefore I tell you, her many sins have been forgiven; that's why she loved much. But the one who is forgiven little, loves little."
    Luke 7:47

✍

Live in harmony with one another. Do not be proud; instead, associate with the humble. Do not be wise in your own estimation. Do not repay anyone evil for evil. Give careful thought to do what is honorable in everyone's eyes. If possible, as far as it depends on you, live at peace with everyone.
    Romans 12:16–18

Be kind and compassionate to one another, forgiving one another, just as God also forgave you in Christ.
    Ephesians 4:32

As God's chosen ones, holy and dearly loved, put on compassion, kindness, humility, gentleness, and patience, bearing with one another and forgiving one another if anyone has a grievance against another. Just as the Lord has forgiven you, so you are also to forgive.
    Colossians 3:12–13

Dear God, just as You forgave all my debts and wrongs through Christ, empower me to extend forgiveness to anyone who has hurt me.

FRIENDSHIP

Precious are the friends and colleagues in our lives who faithfully stand by us through joys and sorrows, victories and failures, gains and loss.

Iron sharpens iron,
and one person sharpens another.
       Proverbs 27:17

Two are better than one because they have a good reward for their efforts. For if either falls, his companion can lift him up; but pity the one who falls without another to lift him up.
       Ecclesiastes 4:9–10

"No one has greater love than this: to lay down his life for his friends. You are my friends if you do what I command you. I do not call you servants anymore, because a servant doesn't know what his master is doing. I have called you friends, because I have made known to you everything I have heard from my Father."
　　John 15:13–15

Dear friends, let us love one another, because love is from God, and everyone who loves has been born of God and knows God.
　　1 John 4:7

Therefore encourage one another and build each other up as you are already doing.
　　1 Thessalonians 5:11

*Lord Jesus, who called His disciples friends,
thank You for demonstrating God's love
for us and how best to love one another.*

GENTLENESS

Gentleness is a gracious approach to others and a demeanor that reigns in strength or assertiveness.

He protects his flock like a shepherd; he gathers the lambs in his arms and carries them in the fold of his garment. He gently leads those that are nursing.
        Isaiah 40:11

Let your graciousness be known to everyone. The Lord is near.
        Philippians 4:5

The Lord's servant must not quarrel, but must be gentle to everyone, able to teach, and patient, instructing his opponents with gentleness.
        2 Timothy 2:24–25

Who among you is wise and understanding? By his good conduct he should show that his works are done in the gentleness that comes from wisdom.

   James 3:13

Lord Jesus, You are the Good Shepherd who demonstrates gentleness to Your people—may Your Spirit inspire in me a gentleness with those I lead.

GRACE

The greatest gift we will ever receive is the wholly unmerited favor of the Most High—let us, therefore, extend this grace to others.

∽

The law came along to multiply the trespass. But where sin multiplied, grace multiplied even more.
   Romans 5:20

∽

For sin will not rule over you, because you are not under the law but under grace.
   Romans 6:14

∽

Now if by grace, then it is not by works; otherwise grace ceases to be grace.
   Romans 11:6

But he said to me, "My grace is sufficient for you, for my power is perfected in weakness." Therefore, I will most gladly boast all the more about my weaknesses, so that Christ's power may reside in me.
    2 Corinthians 12:9

∽

For you are saved by grace through faith, and this is not from yourselves; it is God's gift—not from works, so that no one can boast.
    Ephesians 2:8–9

∽

Lord, thank You for the wealth of grace that has been poured out on me through faith in Christ Jesus.

GREED

When we hoard our possessions, money, food, or other blessings, we reveal a lack of belief that God can and will provide for our needs.

✍

One person gives freely,
yet gains more;
another withholds what is right,
only to become poor.
       Proverbs 11:24

✍

A greedy person stirs up conflict,
but whoever trusts in the LORD will prosper.
       Proverbs 28:25

He then told them, "Watch out and be on guard against all greed,
because one's life is not in the abundance of his possessions."
  Luke 12:15

❧

For the love of money is a root of all kinds of evil, and by craving it, some
have wandered away from the faith and pierced themselves with many
griefs.
  1 Timothy 6:10

❧

Keep your life free from the love of money. Be satisfied with what you
have, for he himself has said, I will never leave you or abandon you.
  Hebrews 13:5

❧

Dear God, please forgive me for any lack
of trust in Your provision, and make me a willing
conduit of Your blessings for those in need.

GRIEF

The deep sorrow that comes from losing a loved one, a longtime friend, or even a leadership position can seem profound and unending—but God promises to be near us, to comfort us, and to bring joy and beauty out of the ashes.

The righteous cry out, and the LORD hears,
and rescues them from all their troubles.
The LORD is near the brokenhearted;
he saves those crushed in spirit.
        Psalm 34:17–18

Then the young women will rejoice with dancing,
while young and old men rejoice together.
I will turn their mourning into joy,
give them consolation,
and bring happiness out of grief.
        Jeremiah 31:13

Why, my soul, are you so dejected?
Why are you in such turmoil?
Put your hope in God, for I will still praise him,
my Savior and my God.
    Psalm 42:5

Though the fig tree does not bud
and there is no fruit on the vines,
though the olive crop fails
and the fields produce no food,
though the flocks disappear from the pen
and there are no herds in the stalls,
yet I will celebrate in the LORD;
I will rejoice in the God of my salvation!
    Habakkuk 3:17–18

Heavenly Father, when my heart
is aching and all I see is darkness, I trust
that You are my light and my salvation.

GUILT

We don't have to be consumed with guilt when we commit willful or unintentional sin—we know there is no condemnation for those in Christ Jesus.

❧

As far as the east is from the west,
so far has he removed
our transgressions from us.
    Psalm 103:12

❧

"Come, let us settle this,"
says the LORD.
"Though your sins are scarlet,
they will be as white as snow;
though they are crimson red,
they will be like wool."
    Isaiah 1:18

Therefore, there is now no condemnation for those in Christ Jesus, because the law of the Spirit of life in Christ Jesus has set you free from the law of sin and death.
Romans 8:1–2

∽

In him we have redemption through his blood, the forgiveness of our trespasses, according to the riches of his grace.
Ephesians 1:7

∽

If we confess our sins, he is faithful and righteous to forgive us our sins and to cleanse us from all unrighteousness.
1 John 1:9

∽

Lord, when I have fallen short of Your glory, grant me wisdom to confess my wrongdoings and be cleansed of all unrighteousness.

HAPPINESS

The great king David wrote in the psalms, "Happy are the people whose God is the LORD" (Ps. 144:15).

❧

Therefore my heart is glad
and my whole being rejoices;
my body also rests securely.
Psalm 16:9

❧

Take delight in the LORD,
and he will give you your heart's desires.
Psalm 37:4

A joyful heart makes a face cheerful,
but a sad heart produces a broken spirit.
Proverbs 15:13

∽

I know that there is nothing better for them than to rejoice and enjoy the good life.
Ecclesiastes 3:12

∽

Rejoice in the Lord always. I will say it again: Rejoice!
Philippians 4:4

∽

Lord, may my heart be happy and cheerful because I know You and can trust in Your strength and guidance.

HOPE

Rather than place our hope in our own strength and abilities, hope instead in our Good Shepherd, Christ Jesus.

But those who trust in the LORD
will renew their strength;
they will soar on wings like eagles;
they will run and not become weary,
they will walk and not faint.
     Isaiah 40:31

We have also obtained access through him by faith into this grace in
which we stand, and we rejoice in the hope of the glory of God. And not
only that, but we also rejoice in our afflictions, because we know that
affliction produces endurance, endurance produces proven character,
and proven character produces hope.
     Romans 5:2–4

I wait for the LORD; I wait
and put my hope in his word.
Psalm 130:5

Now may the God of hope fill you with all joy and peace as you believe
so that you may overflow with hope by the power of the Holy Spirit.
Romans 15:13

Let us run with endurance the race that lies before us, keeping our eyes
on Jesus, the source and perfecter of our faith. For the joy that lay before
him, he endured the cross, despising the shame, and sat down at the
right hand of the throne of God. For consider him who endured such
hostility from sinners against himself, so that you won't grow weary and
give up.
Hebrews 12:1–3

Heavenly Father, please fill me with
all joy and peace as I hope in You.

HUMILITY

The best leaders are those who focus less on themselves and their own abilities and more on building up and supporting the people around them.

❧

Sitting down, he called the Twelve and said to them, "If anyone wants to be first, he must be last and servant of all."
  Mark 9:35

❧

Live in harmony with one another. Do not be proud; instead, associate with the humble. Do not be wise in your own estimation.
  Romans 12:16

❧

Do nothing out of selfish ambition or conceit, but in humility consider others as more important than yourselves.
  Philippians 2:3

Adopt the same attitude as that of Christ Jesus, who, existing in the form of God, did not consider equality with God as something to be exploited. Instead he emptied himself by assuming the form of a servant, taking on the likeness of humanity. And when he had come as a man, he humbled himself by becoming obedient to the point of death—even to death on a cross.

Philippians 2:5–8

∾

Who among you is wise and understanding? By his good conduct he should show that his works are done in the gentleness that comes from wisdom.

James 3:13

∾

Lord Jesus, who demonstrated perfect humility, may my mind be filled with thoughts of You and of others so that I forget myself completely.

IMPULSIVENESS

The feeling that most reliably follows an impulsive word or action is regret—choose instead to be patient and deliberate.

∽

Discretion will watch over you,
and understanding will guard you.
It will rescue you from the way of evil—
from anyone who says perverse things,
    Proverbs 2:11–12

∽

So if you have been raised with Christ, seek the things above, where Christ is, seated at the right hand of God. Set your minds on things above, not on earthly things.
    Colossians 3:1–2

For we all stumble in many ways. If anyone does not stumble in what he says, he is mature, able also to control the whole body.

James 3:2

✐

Watch yourselves so you don't lose what we have worked for, but that you may receive a full reward. Anyone who does not remain in Christ's teaching but goes beyond it does not have God. The one who remains in that teaching, this one has both the Father and the Son.

2 John 8–9

✐

Lord God, I am confident that I will see Your goodness in the land of the living—may Your Spirit empower me to be strong and wait for You.

INTEGRITY

Godly leadership requires that you be consistent in your values, decisions, behaviors, and speech.

The one who lives with integrity lives securely,
but whoever perverts his ways will be found out.
>   Proverbs 10:9

Better the poor person who lives with integrity
than the rich one who distorts right and wrong.
>   Proverbs 28:6

Indeed, we are giving careful thought to do what is right, not only before
the Lord but also before people.
>   2 Corinthians 8:21

Whatever you do, do it from the heart, as something done for the Lord and not for people, knowing that you will receive the reward of an inheritance from the Lord. You serve the Lord Christ.
    Colossians 3:23–24

∽

Yet do this with gentleness and respect, keeping a clear conscience, so that when you are accused, those who disparage your good conduct in Christ will be put to shame.
    1 Peter 3:16

∽

*Lord, may Your Holy Spirit keep fierce
watch over my heart so that I remain
honest and incorruptible, for Your glory.*

JOY

Happiness can be fleeting, but joy is steadfast because it comes from the firm foundation of our intimacy with Christ.

✑

You reveal the path of life to me;
in your presence is abundant joy;
at your right hand are eternal pleasures.
Psalm 16:11

✑

This is the day the LORD has made;
let us rejoice and be glad in it.
Psalm 118:24

But the fruit of the Spirit is love, joy, peace, patience, kindness, goodness, faithfulness, gentleness, and self-control. The law is not against such things.

    Galatians 5:22–23

✍

"As the Father has loved me, I have also loved you. Remain in my love. If you keep my commands you will remain in my love, just as I have kept my Father's commands and remain in his love. I have told you these things so that my joy may be in you and your joy may be complete."

    John 15:9–11

✍

Dear Jesus, thank You for the abundant joy that comes from Your faithful presence.

KINDNESS

In God's great kindness, He saved us through His beloved Son, and He now calls us to extend that same gentleness and compassion to others.

He also raised us up with him and seated us with him in the heavens in Christ Jesus, so that in the coming ages he might display the immeasurable riches of his grace through his kindness to us in Christ Jesus.
　　Ephesians 2:6–7

Let all bitterness, anger and wrath, shouting and slander be removed from you, along with all malice. And be kind and compassionate to one another, forgiving one another, just as God also forgave you in Christ.
　　Ephesians 4:31–32

Therefore, as God's chosen ones, holy and dearly loved, put on compassion, kindness, humility, gentleness, and patience.
Colossians 3:12

∽

But when the kindness of God our Savior and his love for mankind appeared, he saved us—not by works of righteousness that we had done, but according to his mercy—through the washing of regeneration and renewal by the Holy Spirit.
Titus 3:4–5

∽

Dear God, may Your Holy Spirit soften my speech and actions so that I display Your kindness toward my staff and others under my leadership.

KNOWLEDGE

As a leader, you may have a wealth of knowledge and experience, but the deepest knowledge is awe and reverence for the Creator.

∽

For wisdom will enter your heart,
and knowledge will delight you.
> Proverbs 2:10

∽

The mind of the discerning acquires knowledge,
and the ear of the wise seeks it.
> Proverbs 18:15

∽

For the earth will be filled with the knowledge of the LORD's glory, as the
water covers the sea.
> Habakkuk 2:14

We know that "we all have knowledge." Knowledge puffs up, but love builds up. If anyone thinks he knows anything, he does not yet know it as he ought to know it. But if anyone loves God, he is known by him.

1 Corinthians 8:1–3

❧

For this reason also, since the day we heard this, we haven't stopped praying for you. We are asking that you may be filled with the knowledge of his will in all wisdom and spiritual understanding, so that you may walk worthy of the Lord, fully pleasing to him: bearing fruit in every good work and growing in the knowledge of God, being strengthened with all power, according to his glorious might, so that you may have great endurance and patience, joyfully giving thanks to the Father, who has enabled you to share in the saints' inheritance in the light.

Colossians 1:9–12

❧

Lord, may Your Spirit teach me Your Word
and guide me in Your perfect ways.

LAZINESS

Work of all kinds is a gift from God to provide us with not only a living but also a sense of purpose and service to others.

∽

The slacker craves, yet has nothing,
but the diligent is fully satisfied.
    Proverbs 13:4

∽

The one who is lazy in his work
is brother to a vandal.
    Proverbs 18:9

Whatever you do, do it from the heart, as something done for the Lord and not for people, knowing that you will receive the reward of an inheritance from the Lord. You serve the Lord Christ.
Colossians 3:23–24

∽

In fact, when we were with you, this is what we commanded you: "If anyone isn't willing to work, he should not eat."
2 Thessalonians 3:10

∽

Lord, when I'm feeling weary and tired, please strengthen me with the power of Your Holy Spirit.

LEADERSHIP

A true leader isn't one who has climbed to the top of a hierarchy, but one who chooses above all else to be a servant to all.

Jesus called them over and said, "You know that the rulers of the Gentiles lord it over them, and those in high positions act as tyrants over them. It must not be like that among you. On the contrary, whoever wants to become great among you must be your servant, and whoever wants to be first among you must be your slave; just as the Son of Man did not come to be served, but to serve, and to give his life as a ransom for many."
  Matthew 20:25–28

Shepherd God's flock among you, not overseeing out of compulsion but willingly, as God would have you; not out of greed for money but eagerly; not lording it over those entrusted to you, but being examples to the flock. And when the chief Shepherd appears, you will receive the unfading crown of glory.
  1 Peter 5:2–4

Adopt the same attitude as that of Christ Jesus, who, existing in the form of God, did not consider equality with God as something to be exploited. Instead he emptied himself by assuming the form of a servant, taking on the likeness of humanity. And when he had come as a man, he humbled himself by becoming obedient to the point of death—even to death on a cross. For this reason God highly exalted him and gave him the name that is above every name, so that at the name of Jesus every knee will bow—in heaven and on earth and under the earth—and every tongue will confess that Jesus Christ is Lord, to the glory of God the Father.
    Philippians 2:5–11

Don't let anyone despise your youth, but set an example for the believers in speech, in conduct, in love, in faith, and in purity.
    1 Timothy 4:12

*Lord Jesus, You came not to be served
but to serve; grant me Your Spirit
of servant leadership in my endeavors.*

LONELINESS

The loneliness of being a leader is well known—but when you remove the mantle of leadership, you remain a believer with a family and a community to love you and uphold you.

❧

"My presence will go with you, and I will give you rest."
   Exodus 33:14

❧

The LORD is the one who will go before you. He will be with you; he will not leave you or abandon you. Do not be afraid or discouraged.
   Deuteronomy 31:8

❧

God provides homes for those who are deserted.
He leads out the prisoners to prosperity,
but the rebellious live in a scorched land.
   Psalm 68:6

He heals the brokenhearted
and bandages their wounds.
    Psalm 147:3

Blessed be the God and Father of our Lord Jesus Christ, the Father of mercies and the God of all comfort. He comforts us in all our affliction, so that we may be able to comfort those who are in any kind of affliction, through the comfort we ourselves receive from God.
    2 Corinthians 1:3–4

Father of mercies, please comfort me
in times of loneliness so that I may be an
overflowing well of Your love in my daily life.

MERCY

When the demands of leadership get too overwhelming, you can approach God's throne of grace with boldness, and He will give you peace.

"Blessed are the merciful, for they will be shown mercy."
  Matthew 5:7

"Go and learn what this means: I desire mercy and not sacrifice. For I didn't come to call the righteous, but sinners."
  Matthew 9:13

Therefore, let us approach the throne of grace with boldness, so that we may receive mercy and find grace to help us in time of need.
  Hebrews 4:16

Speak and act as those who are to be judged by the law of freedom. For judgment is without mercy to the one who has not shown mercy. Mercy triumphs over judgment.

James 2:12–13

✑

Blessed be the God and Father of our Lord Jesus Christ. Because of his great mercy he has given us new birth into a living hope through the resurrection of Jesus Christ from the dead.

1 Peter 1:3

✑

Lord God, thank You for Your mercy and lovingkindness in times of need.

MONEY

Money is an essential and valuable tool, but too much trust in it or desire for it can quickly lead us away from what's most important.

❧

"No one can serve two masters, since either he will hate one and love the other, or he will be devoted to one and despise the other. You cannot serve both God and money."
   Matthew 6:24

❧

Pay your obligations to everyone: taxes to those you owe taxes, tolls to those you owe tolls, respect to those you owe respect, and honor to those you owe honor.
   Romans 13:7

For the love of money is a root of all kinds of evil, and by craving it, some have wandered away from the faith and pierced themselves with many griefs.
        1 Timothy 6:10

✍

Instruct those who are rich in the present age not to be arrogant or to set their hope on the uncertainty of wealth, but on God, who richly provides us with all things to enjoy.
        1 Timothy 6:17

✍

Keep your life free from the love of money. Be satisfied with what you have, for he himself has said, "I will never leave you or abandon you."
        Hebrews 13:5

✍

Heavenly Father, who richly provides us with so much abundance, please keep my heart free from covetousness and the love of money.

MOTIVES

Rather than self-seeking or people-pleasing, leaders should endeavor to pursue their mission with genuine love for God and others.

∽

But the LORD said to Samuel, "Do not look at his appearance or his stature because I have rejected him. Humans do not see what the LORD sees, for humans see what is visible, but the LORD sees the heart."
    1 Samuel 16:7

∽

All a person's ways seem right to him,
but the LORD weighs hearts.
    Proverbs 21:2

For am I now trying to persuade people, or God? Or am I striving to please people? If I were still trying to please people, I would not be a servant of Christ.
    Galatians 1:10

∽

Do nothing out of selfish ambition or conceit, but in humility consider others as more important than yourselves.
    Philippians 2:3

∽

Instead, just as we have been approved by God to be entrusted with the gospel, so we speak, not to please people, but rather God, who examines our hearts.
    1 Thessalonians 2:4

∽

Lord, please weigh my heart and my reasons for doing the things I do, and reveal to me any motives that don't glorify You.

OBEDIENCE

Obedience means yielding to the will of God, which is to love Him with all of your heart, soul, and mind, and to love your neighbor as yourself.

❧

I have chosen the way of truth;
I have set your ordinances before me.
    Psalm 119:30

❧

"If you love me, you will keep my commands."
    John 14:15

❧

Peter and the apostles replied, "We must obey God rather than people."
    Acts 5:29

The one who keeps his commands remains in him, and he in him. And the way we know that he remains in us is from the Spirit he has given us.
    1 John 3:24

∽

For this is what love for God is: to keep his commands. And his commands are not a burden, because everyone who has been born of God conquers the world. This is the victory that has conquered the world: our faith.
    1 John 5:3–4

∽

Lord, may Your Spirit guide me in all my thoughts, words, and actions so that I am fully submitted to Your will.

PATIENCE

Given the myriad pressures and uncertainty that are present in managing a group of people, a godly leader is one who can remain patient even in trying times.

✺

The end of a matter is better than its beginning; a patient spirit is better than a proud spirit.
> *Ecclesiastes 7:8*

✺

Now if we hope for what we do not see, we eagerly wait for it with patience.
> *Romans 8:25*

✺

My dear brothers and sisters, understand this: Everyone should be quick to listen, slow to speak, and slow to anger, for human anger does not accomplish God's righteousness.
> *James 1:19–20*

Therefore, brothers and sisters, be patient until the Lord's coming. See how the farmer waits for the precious fruit of the earth and is patient with it until it receives the early and the late rains. You also must be patient. Strengthen your hearts, because the Lord's coming is near.
James 5:7–8

The Lord does not delay his promise, as some understand delay, but is patient with you, not wanting any to perish but all to come to repentance.
2 Peter 3:9

Lord God, Your mercies are new every morning— please grant me a spirit of patience with my staff and others in my organization.

POWER

A leader's greatest power lies in his or her ability to submit to the wisdom and guidance of the Holy Spirit within.

❧

"But you will receive power when the Holy Spirit has come on you, and you will be my witnesses in Jerusalem, in all Judea and Samaria, and to the end of the earth."
    Acts 1:8

❧

For the kingdom of God is not a matter of talk but of power.
    1 Corinthians 4:20

But he said to me, "My grace is sufficient for you, for my power is perfected in weakness."
Therefore, I will most gladly boast all the more about my weaknesses, so that Christ's power may reside in me.
2 Corinthians 12:9

For God has not given us a spirit of fear, but one of power, love, and sound judgment.
2 Timothy 1:7

Dear Jesus, when I feel weak or powerless,
I look to You for Your grace and strength.

PRAYER

Whether we come to present our requests or just to sit silently in His presence, prayer is an essential daily spiritual practice.

"If you remain in me and my words remain in you, ask whatever you want and it will be done for you."
    John 15:7

In the same way the Spirit also helps us in our weakness, because we do not know what to pray for as we should, but the Spirit himself intercedes for us with unspoken groanings.
    Romans 8:26

Don't worry about anything, but in everything, through prayer and petition with thanksgiving, present your requests to God.
    Philippians 4:6

"Whenever you pray, you must not be like the hypocrites, because they love to pray standing in the synagogues and on the street corners to be seen by people. Truly I tell you, they have their reward. But when you pray, go into your private room, shut your door, and pray to your Father who is in secret. And your Father who sees in secret will reward you. When you pray, don't babble like the Gentiles, since they imagine they'll be heard for their many words. Don't be like them, because your Father knows the things you need before you ask him.

"Therefore, you should pray like this: Our Father in heaven, your name be honored as holy. Your kingdom come. Your will be done on earth as it is in heaven. Give us today our daily bread. And forgive us our debts, as we also have forgiven our debtors. And do not bring us into temptation, but deliver us from the evil one.

"For if you forgive others their offenses, your heavenly Father will forgive you as well. But if you don't forgive others, your Father will not forgive your offenses."

Matthew 6:5–15

∽

Pray constantly.

1 Thessalonians 5:17

∽

Lord Jesus, just as You taught your followers how to pray, instill in me a deep desire to seek Your presence.

PRIDE

Though we may be blessed with wisdom and success, we can avoid arrogance by remembering that our position in leadership is service to God.

∽

When arrogance comes, disgrace follows,
but with humility comes wisdom.
        Proverbs 11:2

∽

Everyone with a proud heart is detestable to the LORD;
be assured, he will not go unpunished.
        Proverbs 16:5

∽

A person's pride will humble him,
but a humble spirit will gain honor.
        Proverbs 29:23

Live in harmony with one another. Do not be proud; instead, associate with the humble. Do not be wise in your own estimation.
　　Romans 12:16

∽

For if anyone considers himself to be something when he is nothing, he deceives himself.
　　Galatians 6:3

∽

Father God, please forgive the ways I puff myself up rather than humble myself under Your loving hand.

PURPOSE

Our deepest purpose is not in what we do but in who we are—people who love, honor, and praise God.

When all has been heard, the conclusion of the matter is this: fear God and keep his commands, because this is for all humanity.
  Ecclesiastes 12:13

"My Father is glorified by this: that you produce much fruit and prove to be my disciples."
  John 15:8

But I consider my life of no value to myself; my purpose is to finish my course and the ministry I received from the Lord Jesus, to testify to the gospel of God's grace.
  Acts 20:24

He has saved us and called us with a holy calling, not according to our works, but according to his own purpose and grace, which was given to us in Christ Jesus before time began.
     2 Timothy 1:9

∽

Sing to him; sing praise to him; tell about all his wondrous works! Honor his holy name; let the hearts of those who seek the LORD rejoice.
     1 Chronicles 16:9–10

∽

Lord Jesus, may each day offer me opportunities
to live out my truest purpose by loving and
serving You and those around me.

RELIABILITY

The reliability of a leader will define the stability of a healthy organizational culture—it is a demonstration of God's own character.

❧

He will not allow your foot to slip;
your Protector will not slumber.
     Psalm 121:3

❧

"But let your 'yes' mean 'yes,' and your 'no' mean 'no.' Anything more
than this is from the evil one."
     Matthew 5:37

"Whoever is faithful in very little is also faithful in much, and whoever is unrighteous in very little is also unrighteous in much."
    Luke 16:10

What you have heard from me in the presence of many witnesses, commit to faithful men who will be able to teach others also.
    2 Timothy 2:2

Lord, just as You are constant and faithful, help me to be a leader that my people can reliably depend upon.

RIGHTEOUSNESS

God made the one who knew no sin to be sin for us, so that in Him we might become the very righteousness of God.

How happy are those who uphold justice,
who practice righteousness at all times.
    Psalm 106:3

"For I tell you, unless your righteousness surpasses that of the scribes and Pharisees, you will never get into the kingdom of heaven."
    Matthew 5:20

He made the one who did not know sin to be sin for us, so that in him we might become the righteousness of God.
    2 Corinthians 5:21

But even if you should suffer for righteousness, you are blessed. Do not fear what they fear or be intimidated, but in your hearts regard Christ the Lord as holy, ready at any time to give a defense to anyone who asks you for a reason for the hope that is in you.

1 Peter 3:14–15

∽

Children, let no one deceive you. The one who does what is right is righteous, just as he is righteous.

1 John 3:7

∽

Heavenly Father, may Your Spirit guide me and empower me to glorify You by being a leader who does what is right and just.

SACRIFICE

Our willingness to sacrifice our money, possessions, time, energy, and attention attests to our faith in God's abundant provision in all things.

"This is my command: Love one another as I have loved you. No one has greater love than this: to lay down his life for his friends. You are my friends if you do what I command you."
    John 15:12–14

But God proves his own love for us in that while we were still sinners, Christ died for us.
    Romans 5:8

Don't neglect to do what is good and to share, for God is pleased with such sacrifices.
    Hebrews 13:16

When they arrived at the place that God had told him about, Abraham built the altar there and arranged the wood. He bound his son Isaac and placed him on the altar on top of the wood. Then Abraham reached out and took the knife to slaughter his son. But the angel of the LORD called to him from heaven and said, "Abraham, Abraham!" He replied, "Here I am."

Then he said, "Do not lay a hand on the boy or do anything to him. For now I know that you fear God, since you have not withheld your only son from me." Abraham looked up and saw a ram caught in the thicket by its horns. So Abraham went and took the ram and offered it as a burnt offering in place of his son. And Abraham named that place The LORD Will Provide, so today it is said: "It will be provided on the LORD's mountain."

Then the angel of the LORD called to Abraham a second time from heaven and said, "By myself I have sworn," this is the LORD's declaration: "Because you have done this thing and have not withheld your only son, I will indeed bless you and make your offspring as numerous as the stars of the sky and the sand on the seashore. Your offspring will possess the city gates of their enemies. And all the nations of the earth will be blessed by your offspring because you have obeyed my command."

Genesis 22:9–18

Father God, just as You did not withhold Your own Son, grant me a heart willing to give of my gifts and blessings for the good of others.

SAVIOR

Christ Jesus is our Savior, the source and perfecter of our faith, who for the joy set before Him endured the cross.

He said, "They are indeed my people, children who will not be disloyal," and he became their Savior. In all their suffering, he suffered, and the angel of his presence saved them. He redeemed them because of his love and compassion; he lifted them up and carried them all the days of the past.
    Isaiah 63:8–9

My soul praises the greatness of the Lord, and my spirit rejoices in God my Savior, because he has looked with favor on the humble condition of his servant.
    Luke 1:46–48

"This Jesus is the stone rejected by you builders, which has become the cornerstone. There is salvation in no one else, for there is no other name under heaven given to people by which we must be saved."

    Acts 4:11–12

∾

This is good, and it pleases God our Savior, who wants everyone to be saved and to come to the knowledge of the truth.

    1 Timothy 2:3–4

∾

And we have seen and we testify that the Father has sent his Son as the world's Savior.

    1 John 4:14

∾

Lord Jesus, I have been crucified with You—
may the life I now live be lived for You who
loved me and gave Yourself for me.

SELF-CONTROL

We often think of self-control in terms of moral behavior, but consider also the importance of holding our tongues—a leader's speech should be measured and gracious.

✍

A person who does not control his temper
is like a city whose wall is broken down.
    Proverbs 25:28

✍

No temptation has come upon you except what is common to humanity.
But God is faithful; he will not allow you to be tempted beyond what you
are able, but with the temptation he will also provide a way out so that
you may be able to bear it.
    1 Corinthians 10:13

Finally brothers and sisters, whatever is true, whatever is honorable, whatever is just, whatever is pure, whatever is lovely, whatever is commendable—if there is any moral excellence and if there is anything praiseworthy—dwell on these things.
Philippians 4:8

Be sober-minded, be alert. Your adversary the devil is prowling around like a roaring lion, looking for anyone he can devour.
1 Peter 5:8

Lord God, when I struggle with temptation or am quick to anger, please renew Your gentle Spirit within me.

SERVICE

Christ Jesus, the king of heaven, came not to be served but to serve others and set for us His example to follow.

"And the King will answer them, 'Truly I tell you, whatever you did for one of the least of these brothers and sisters of mine, you did for me.'"
Matthew 25:40

"For even the Son of Man did not come to be served, but to serve, and to give his life as a ransom for many."
Mark 10:45

I have been crucified with Christ, and I no longer live, but Christ lives in me. The life I now live in the body, I live by faith in the Son of God, who loved me and gave himself for me.
Galatians 2:20

Therefore, my dear brothers and sisters, be steadfast, immovable,
always excelling in the Lord's work, because you know that your labor
in the Lord is not in vain.
    1 Corinthians 15:58

           ✎

Lord Jesus, please open my eyes to see
the manifold opportunities to serve my staff,
colleagues, and organization, and open
my heart to do so freely and with compassion.

SOVEREIGNTY OF GOD

We trust in God's sovereignty because He is the Creator of the universe and sustains all things by His powerful Word.

❧

The LORD does whatever he pleases
in heaven and on earth,
in the seas and all the depths.
Psalm 135:6

❧

A person's heart plans his way,
but the LORD determines his steps.
Proverbs 16:9

❧

A king's heart is like channeled water in the LORD's hand:
He directs it wherever he chooses.
Proverbs 21:1

What should we say then? Is there injustice with God? Absolutely not! For he tells Moses, I will show mercy to whom I will show mercy, and I will have compassion on whom I will have compassion. So then, it does not depend on human will or effort but on God who shows mercy. For the Scripture tells Pharaoh, I raised you up for this reason so that I may display my power in you and that my name may be proclaimed in the whole earth. So then, he has mercy on whom he wants to have mercy and he hardens whom he wants to harden.

    Romans 9:14–18

§

We know that all things work together for the good of those who love God, who are called according to his purpose.

    Romans 8:28

§

*Good and faithful God, may my heart and
soul rest in knowing that You uphold the world
and Your purposes cannot be thwarted.*

SPEECH

When we speak, the words we choose are only part of our response—we must also consider our motives and tone of voice.

A gentle answer turns away anger,
but a harsh word stirs up wrath.
    Proverbs 15:1

Let your speech always be gracious, seasoned with salt, so that you may know how you should answer each person.
    Colossians 4:6

Bless those who persecute you; bless and do not curse.
    Romans 12:14

But no one can tame the tongue. It is a restless evil, full of deadly poison. With the tongue we bless our Lord and Father, and with it we curse people who are made in God's likeness. Blessing and cursing come out of the same mouth. My brothers and sisters, these things should not be this way.

James 3:8–10

No foul language should come from your mouth, but only what is good for building up someone in need, so that it gives grace to those who hear.

Ephesians 4:29

Holy Spirit, please fill my heart with the gracious love of God so that my speech is humble, gentle, and kind.

STRENGTH

A leader's greatest source of strength is trusting in the power and love of God, who provides grace in times of need.

❧

My flesh and my heart may fail,
but God is the strength of my heart,
my portion forever.
Psalm 73:26

❧

If I say, "My foot is slipping,"
your faithful love will support me, LORD.
Psalm 94:18

But he said to me, "My grace is sufficient for you, for my power is perfected in weakness." Therefore, I will most gladly boast all the more about my weaknesses, so that Christ's power may reside in me. So I take pleasure in weaknesses, insults, hardships, persecutions, and in difficulties, for the sake of Christ. For when I am weak, then I am strong.

2 Corinthians 12:9–10

❧

Consider it a great joy, my brothers and sisters, whenever you experience various trials, because you know that the testing of your faith produces endurance.

James 1:2–3

❧

Lord Jesus, Your grace is sufficient for me—
may your power be perfected in my
moments of weakness and exhaustion.

STRESS

Being a leader means shouldering immense responsibilities and the success of the organization. When you feel overwhelmed, remember that God is an ever-present helper in times of trouble.

&

Cast your burden on the LORD,
and he will sustain you;
he will never allow the righteous to be shaken.
    Psalm 55:22

&

Commit your activities to the LORD,
and your plans will be established.
    Proverbs 16:3

For I am the LORD your God, who holds your right hand, who says to you, "Do not fear, I will help you."
    Isaiah 41:13

⤷∽

"Come to me, all of you who are weary and burdened, and I will give you rest. Take up my yoke and learn from me, because I am lowly and humble in heart, and you will find rest for your souls. For my yoke is easy and my burden is light."
    Matthew 11:28–30

⤷∽

I am able to do all things through him who strengthens me.
    Philippians 4:13

⤷∽

Dear God, please strengthen me by Your Spirit when I feel overwhelmed, exhausted, and uncertain.

SUCCESS

Whether you succeed or fail at leading your group or organization, your true identity is your relationship with the Lord Jesus.

∽

Take delight in the LORD,
and he will give you your heart's desires.
        Psalm 37:4

∽

Commit your activities to the LORD,
and your plans will be established.
        Proverbs 16:3

"For what will it benefit someone if he gains the whole world yet loses his life? Or what will anyone give in exchange for his life? For the Son of Man is going to come with his angels in the glory of his Father, and then he will reward each according to what he has done."
   Matthew 16:26–27

∽

Humble yourselves before the Lord, and he will exalt you.
   James 4:10

∽

Lord Jesus, no matter how well I lead my people or succeed in our goals, help me remember that my purpose is to be a shining beacon of Your light and love.

TEACHING

A wise and mature leader is also a teachable one—someone who not only shares wisdom but also humbly receives good counsel as well.

Until I come, give your attention to public reading, exhortation, and teaching.
    1 Timothy 4:13

Preach the word; be ready in season and out of season; rebuke, correct, and encourage with great patience and teaching.
    2 Timothy 4:2

In the same way, encourage the young men to be self-controlled in everything. Make yourself an example of good works with integrity and dignity in your teaching. Your message is to be sound beyond reproach, so that any opponent will be ashamed, because he doesn't have anything bad to say about us.

Titus 2:6–8

༄

Not many should become teachers, my brothers, because you know that we will receive a stricter judgment.

James 3:1

༄

Heavenly Father, as You have taught me through Your Word, may I both receive and be a source of godly instruction.

TEMPTATION

There are some temptations that are unavoidable. However, God is faithful to provide an escape from what tempts you.

⚭

"Stay awake and pray, so that you won't enter into temptation. The spirit is willing, but the flesh is weak."
   Matthew 26:41

⚭

No temptation has come upon you except what is common to humanity. But God is faithful; he will not allow you to be tempted beyond what you are able, but with the temptation he will also provide a way out so that you may be able to bear it.
   1 Corinthians 10:13

For since he himself has suffered when he was tempted, he is able to help those who are tempted.
Hebrews 2:18

∽

No one undergoing a trial should say, "I am being tempted by God," since God is not tempted by evil, and he himself doesn't tempt anyone. But each person is tempted when he is drawn away and enticed by his own evil desire. Then after desire has conceived, it gives birth to sin, and when sin is fully grown, it gives birth to death.
James 1:13–15

∽

Therefore, submit to God. Resist the devil, and he will flee from you.
James 4:7

∽

Lord God, my spirit is willing, but my flesh is weak—please help me to honor You in all of my choices.

THANKFULNESS

The more we practice gratitude and thanksgiving, the more abundance and goodness we recognize all around us.

⁊

Give thanks to the LORD, for he is good;
his faithful love endures forever.
    Psalm 118:1

⁊

For we know that the one who raised the Lord Jesus will also raise us
with Jesus and present us with you. Indeed, everything is for your benefit
so that, as grace extends through more and more people, it may cause
thanksgiving to increase to the glory of God.
    2 Corinthians 4:14–15

Let the word of Christ dwell richly among you, in all wisdom teaching and admonishing one another through psalms, hymns, and spiritual songs, singing to God with gratitude in your hearts.
    Colossians 3:16

∾

Rejoice always, pray constantly, give thanks in everything; for this is God's will for you in Christ Jesus.
    1 Thessalonians 5:16–18

∾

Every good and perfect gift is from above, coming down from the Father of lights, who does not change like shifting shadows.
    James 1:17

∾

Father of lights, I praise You and thank You for every good and perfect gift You have given.

TRUST

To trust the Lord is to believe what He has said about Himself: He is good, faithful, and sovereign.

The person who trusts in the LORD, whose confidence indeed is the LORD, is blessed. He will be like a tree planted by water: it sends its roots out toward a stream, it doesn't fear when heat comes, and its foliage remains green. It will not worry in a year of drought or cease producing fruit.
  Jeremiah 17:7–8

Wait for the LORD;
be strong, and let your heart be courageous.
Wait for the LORD.
  Psalm 27:14

I will be with you when you pass through the waters, and when you pass through the rivers, they will not overwhelm you. You will not be scorched when you walk through the fire, and the flame will not burn you.

Isaiah 43:2

ॐ

And my God will supply all your needs according to his riches in glory in Christ Jesus.

Philippians 4:19

ॐ

This is the confidence we have before him: If we ask anything according to his will, he hears us.

1 John 5:14

ॐ

Dear God, thank You that all things work together for the good of those who love You and are called according to Your purpose.

VICTORY

You can have joy knowing that it is not up to you to fight all of your battles as a leader, but to rest in the strength and sufficiency of God.

For the LORD your God is the one who goes with you to fight for you against your enemies to give you victory.
    Deuteronomy 20:4

Though a righteous person falls seven times,
he will get up,
but the wicked will stumble into ruin.
    Proverbs 24:16

"I have told you these things so that in me you may have peace. You will have suffering in this world. Be courageous! I have conquered the world."
    John 16:33

The sting of death is sin, and the power of sin is the law. But thanks be to God, who gives us the victory through our Lord Jesus Christ!
    1 Corinthians 15:56–57

Then I heard a loud voice from the throne: Look, God's dwelling is with humanity, and he will live with them. They will be his peoples, and God himself will be with them and will be their God. He will wipe away every tear from their eyes. Death will be no more; grief, crying, and pain will be no more, because the previous things have passed away.
    Revelation 21:3–4

Christ Jesus, it is through You that all of my victories are won—please strengthen me today with a sense of Your presence.

WEALTH

God has provided richly for us with all things to enjoy—therefore let us be gracious and generous toward those in need.

∽

Who do I have in heaven but you?
And I desire nothing on earth but you.
    Psalm 73:25

∽

"Don't store up for yourselves treasures on earth, where moth and rust destroy and where thieves break in and steal. But store up for yourselves treasures in heaven, where neither moth nor rust destroys, and where thieves don't break in and steal."
    Matthew 6:19–20

I know both how to make do with little, and I know how to make do with a lot. In any and all circumstances I have learned the secret of being content—whether well fed or hungry, whether in abundance or in need.
   Philippians 4:12

Instruct those who are rich in the present age not to be arrogant or to set their hope on the uncertainty of wealth, but on God, who richly provides us with all things to enjoy. Instruct them to do what is good, to be rich in good works, to be generous and willing to share, storing up treasure for themselves as a good foundation for the coming age, so that they may take hold of what is truly life.
   1 Timothy 6:17–19

*Lord Jesus, I praise You and thank You
that my richest gain is knowing You.*

WISDOM

Though your leadership may have granted you years of experience, true wisdom comes from the Holy Spirit, who points to what is true, good, and right.

✍

*Teach us to number our days carefully
so that we may develop wisdom in our hearts.*
    Psalm 90:12

✍

*Do not be conformed to this age, but be transformed by the renewing
of your mind, so that you may discern what is the good, pleasing, and
perfect will of God.*
    Romans 12:2

Yet to those who are called, both Jews and Greeks, Christ is the power of God and the wisdom of God, because God's foolishness is wiser than human wisdom, and God's weakness is stronger than human strength.

1 Corinthians 1:24–25

∽

Now if any of you lacks wisdom, he should ask God—who gives to all generously and ungrudgingly—and it will be given to him.

James 1:5

∽

Heavenly Father, who gives generously and freely, please grant me your wisdom to be a godly leader.

WORRY

When we worry, we tend to imagine what might happen but probably won't—Jesus said we cannot add a moment to our lifespan with needless anxiety.

"Therefore I tell you: Don't worry about your life, what you will eat or what you will drink; or about your body, what you will wear. Isn't life more than food and the body more than clothing? Consider the birds of the sky: They don't sow or reap or gather into barns, yet your heavenly Father feeds them. Aren't you worth more than they? Can any of you add one moment to his life-span by worrying?"
    Matthew 6:25–27

The Lord answered her, "Martha, Martha, you are worried and upset about many things, but one thing is necessary. Mary has made the right choice, and it will not be taken away from her."
    Luke 10:41–42

We know that all things work together for the good of those who love God, who are called according to his purpose.
    Romans 8:28

Don't worry about anything, but in everything, through prayer and petition with thanksgiving, present your requests to God. And the peace of God, which surpasses all understanding, will guard your hearts and minds in Christ Jesus.
    Philippians 4:6–7

Lord Jesus, I am often worried about many things—please grant me a heart like Mary, who rested at Your feet.

VERSE INDEX